MY DAD
A PHOTOLOG BOOK

Created by Janet Horowitz and Kathy Faggella

Illustrated by Steve Jenkins

Stewart, Tabori & Chang
New York

Published and distributed in the U.S. by Stewart, Tabori & Chang,
575 Broadway, New York, NY 10012.
Distributed in Canada by General Publishing Company Limited,
30 Lesmill Road, Don Mills, Ontario, Canada, M3B 2T6.
Distributed in the U.K. by Hi Marketing, 38 Carver Road,
London SE24 9LT, England.
Distributed in Europe by Onslow Books Limited, Tyler's Court,
111A Wardour Street, London W1V 3TD, England.
Distributed in Australia and New Zealand by Peribo Pty Limited,
58 Beaumont Road, Mount Kuring-gai NSW 2080.

Printed in Singapore

First Printed 1991

10 9 8 7 6 5 4 3

Your dad is an important person in your life. You probably know him very well, but wouldn't it be fun to know more about him? Wouldn't it be interesting to know what his favorite things are, and in which ways you are alike? Wouldn't it be fun to be able to give your opinions and comments about Dad as you see him?

You can! Here is the opportunity for you to have fun as you get to know your dad even better. With this book, a camera, film, and a little time spent with Dad, you can learn a lot about him and about yourself as well. You can be a photographer, reporter, and writer of your own PhotoLog book about you and your dad.

Uses for your **My Dad** book:

• Use **My Dad** as an ice breaker—it will open up discussions and conversations with Dad and the whole family.

• Use **My Dad** to think about comparisons between your life and your dad's, the ways you are alike and how you differ. Maybe you can find the reasons why this is so.

• Use **My Dad** to make connections with your dad. When you realize that you enjoy the same things, you can do them together.

• Use **My Dad** as a gift for your dad. He would be thrilled to have a book written all about him (and you)!

• Use **My Dad** as a treasured memory book, to help you remember all the special times you spent together with your dad.

Some hints to help you complete your book:

1. Take photos.
Be prepared to take photos of your dad that will fit the photo captions. One roll of 24-print film will be enough for this book. Try and take candid photos of your dad. You will also need two old photos of Dad.

2. Talk with your dad.
In between the picture taking, interview Dad about the things that you notice. Ask questions when you think of them or write them down so that you won't forget to ask him later. Listen carefully to the things your dad tells you and others. Listen to the stories that friends and relatives tell you about your dad.

3. Fill in this book.
When your pictures are ready, decide which ones would best fit the photo captions and pages of this book. Then complete the pages. Some answers can be found by watching and observing, others from talking with your dad. Follow the order in this book, or skip around, whatever makes you feel comfortable. You do not have to fill in everything. And remember, have fun!

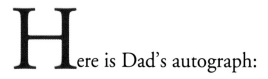

_____

H ere is Dad's autograph:

_____

Dad's autograph makes me think that he's:

☐ formal   ☐ mysterious   ☐ tired
☐ shy   ☐ artistic   ☐ absent-minded
☐ self-confident ☐ messy   ☐ _____

and he really is _____.

Here is my autograph:

_____

MY DAD

W

hat Dad remembers best about his mom (my grandma _____) is _____
    her name
_____ .

What Dad remembers best about his dad (my grandpa _ _____) is _____
    his name
_____ .

Dad has one word about his family:_____ .

_____

Dad grew up in _____.

His favorite childhood game was _____

His best toy was _____

He had a pet _____ named _____

Dad spent a lot of his time _____

_____

DAD AS A KID

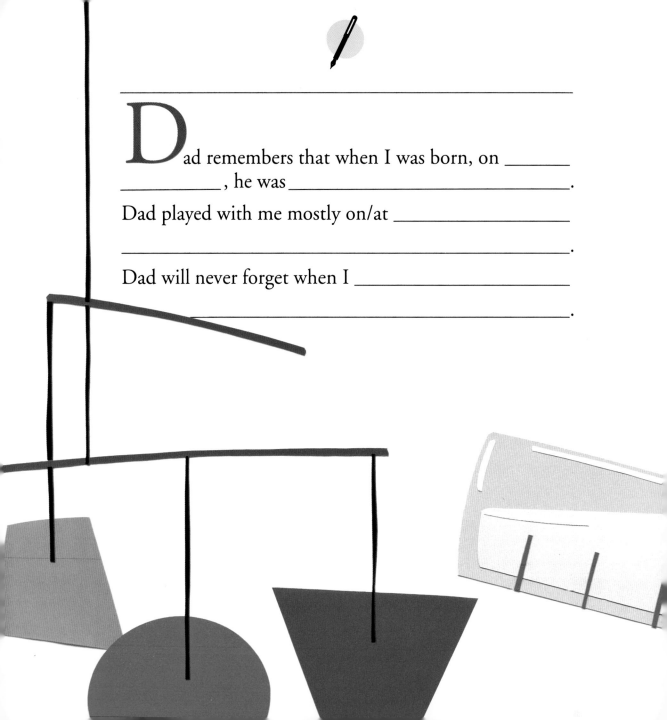

Dad remembers that when I was born, on _____
_____ , he was _____ .

Dad played with me mostly on/at _____

_____ .

Dad will never forget when I _____

_____ .

DAD WITH ME AS A BABY

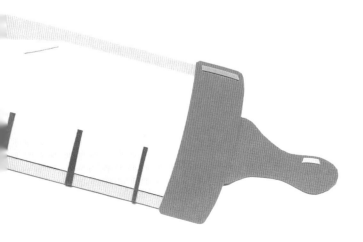

Together, Dad and I like to _____

_____

_____.

Together, on weekends, we _____

_____.

Together, we've made _____.

Together, we've traveled to _____.

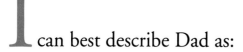

I can best describe Dad as:

☐ funny   ☐ patient   ☐ serious
☐ adventurous   ☐ sociable   ☐ intelligent
☐ musical   ☐ artistic   ☐ active
☐ grumpy   ☐ relaxed   ☐ _____

If Dad were an animal, he'd be a _____.

If Dad were a toy, he'd be a _____.

If Dad were a car, he'd be a _____.

If Dad were a TV character, he'd be _____.

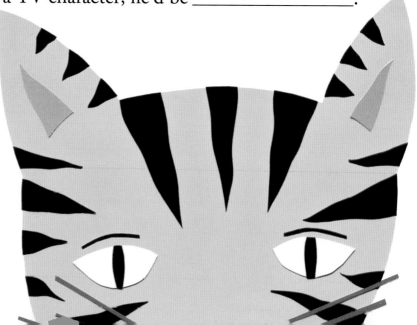

Check the places where you might find Dad:

☐ the yard   ☐ the kitchen   ☐ on the phone
☐ the basement   ☐ the bedroom   ☐ the computer
☐ the golf course   ☐ on the road   ☐ the stores
☐ the bathroom   ☐ the garage   ☐ the park
☐ his chair   ☐ by the TV   ☐ _____

Go back and put an X on the places where you'd never find Dad.

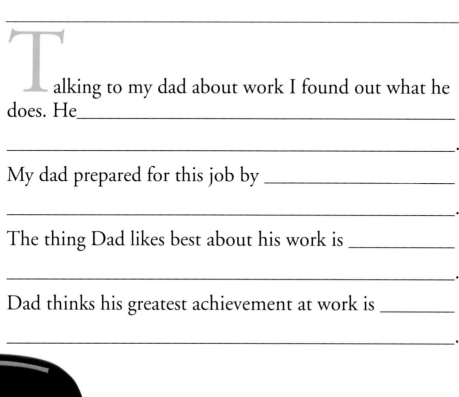

Talking to my dad about work I found out what he does. He_____
_____.

My dad prepared for this job by _____
_____.

The thing Dad likes best about his work is _____
_____.

Dad thinks his greatest achievement at work is _____
_____.

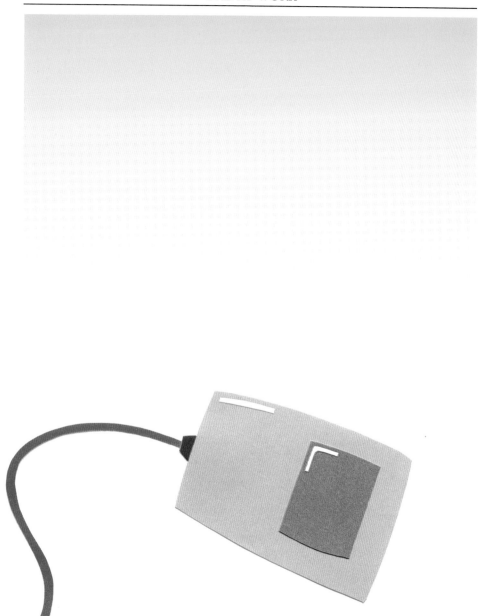

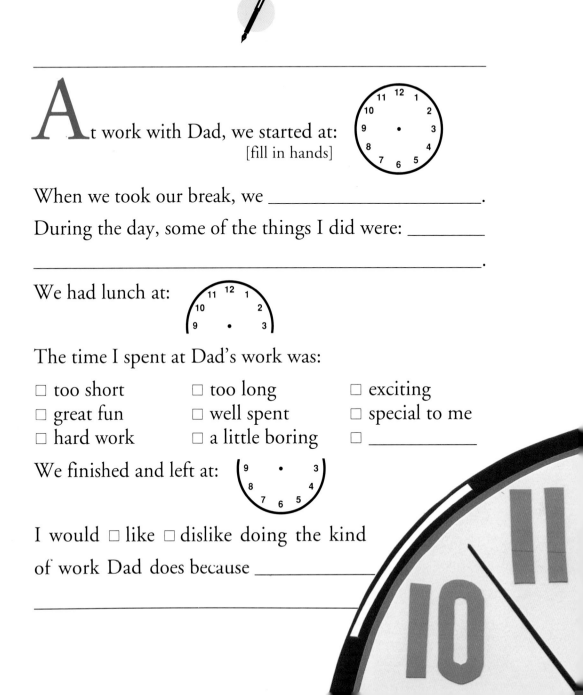

At work with Dad, we started at:
[fill in hands]

When we took our break, we _____.

During the day, some of the things I did were: _____

_____.

We had lunch at:

The time I spent at Dad's work was:

☐ too short   ☐ too long   ☐ exciting
☐ great fun   ☐ well spent   ☐ special to me
☐ hard work   ☐ a little boring   ☐ _____

We finished and left at:

I would ☐ like ☐ dislike doing the kind

of work Dad does because _____

_____

The first thing Dad likes to do at home is _____

_____.

Dad would like to spend his time _____

_____.

Dad actually spends his time _____

_____.

When Dad's home we _____

_____.

Eating with Dad usually means:

☐ snacking when hungry
☐ eating on the go
☐ sitting in front of the TV
☐ having formal sit-down meals
☐ having fast foods
☐ going out to restaurants
☐ having lively table talk
☐ having lots of good food

Our favorite meal is _____

_____ .

DAD EATING

Dad's favorite sport to play is _____.

Dad's favorite sport to watch is _____.

Dad's favorite team is _____.

Dad also exercises by _____
_____.

Dad would like to learn how to _____
_____.

Together Dad and I like to play _____
_____

Dad's toys are _____
_____.
My toys are _____
_____.
Dad would like a new _____.
I would like a new _____.

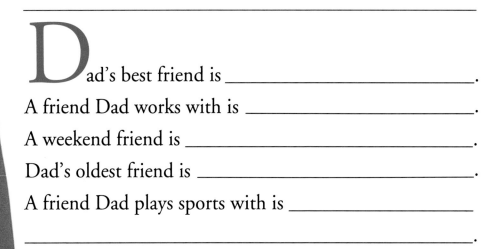

Dad's best friend is _____.

A friend Dad works with is _____.

A weekend friend is _____.

Dad's oldest friend is _____.

A friend Dad plays sports with is _____

_____.

Happiness for Dad is _____
_____.

Dad is happy when I _____
_____.

Dad is happy in this photo because____
_____.

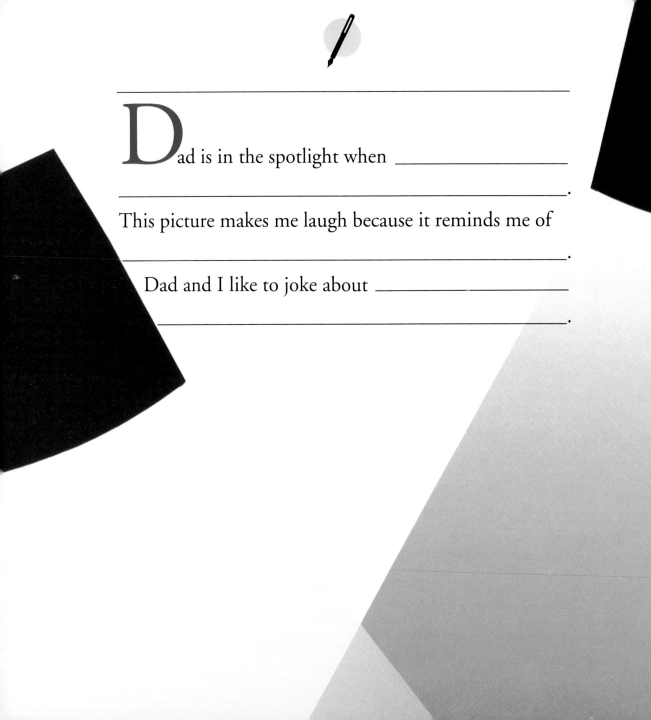

Dad is in the spotlight when _____

_____.

This picture makes me laugh because it reminds me of

_____.

Dad and I like to joke about _____

_____.

When Dad and I go out together, we go to _____
_____.

I wish we could also _____
_____.

If I had one wish for a fantasy vacation it would be _____
_____
_____.

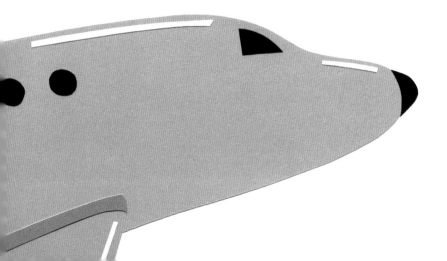

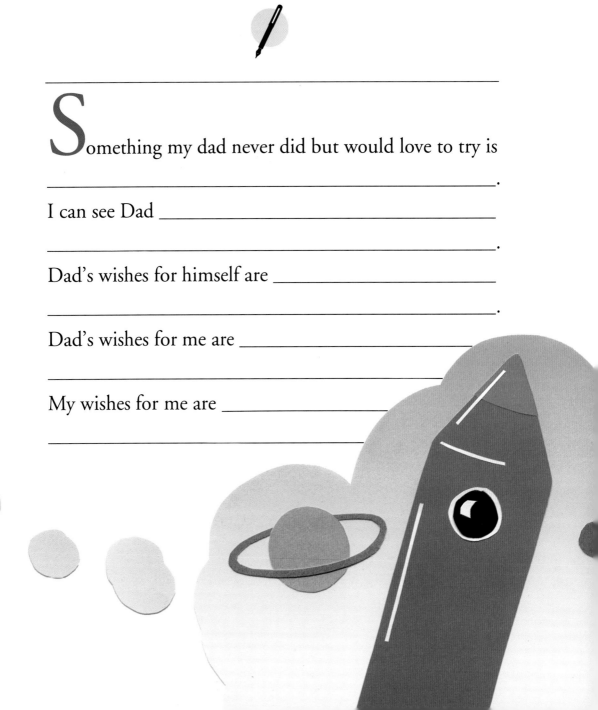

Something my dad never did but would love to try is
_____.

I can see Dad _____
_____.

Dad's wishes for himself are _____
_____.

Dad's wishes for me are _____
_____

My wishes for me are _____
_____

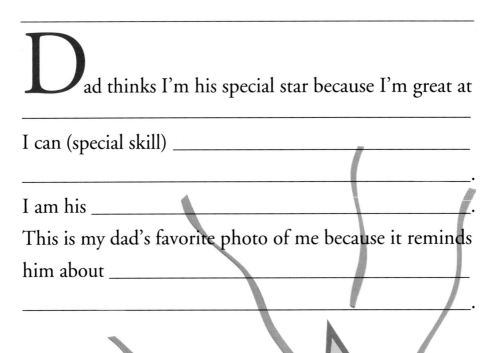

Dad thinks I'm his special star because I'm great at

_____

I can (special skill) _____

_____.

I am his _____.

This is my dad's favorite photo of me because it reminds

him about _____

_____.

DAD'S FAVORITE PHOTO OF ME

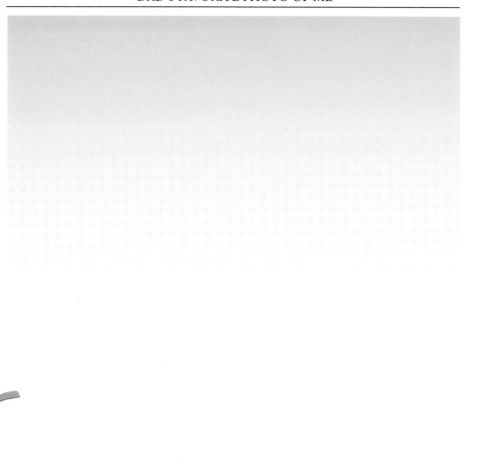

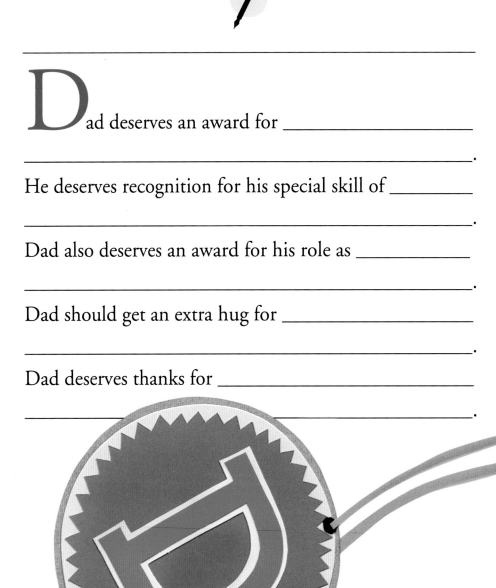

Dad deserves an award for _____
_____.

He deserves recognition for his special skill of _____
_____.

Dad also deserves an award for his role as _____
_____.

Dad should get an extra hug for _____
_____.

Dad deserves thanks for _____
_____.

AN AWARD I MADE FOR DAD

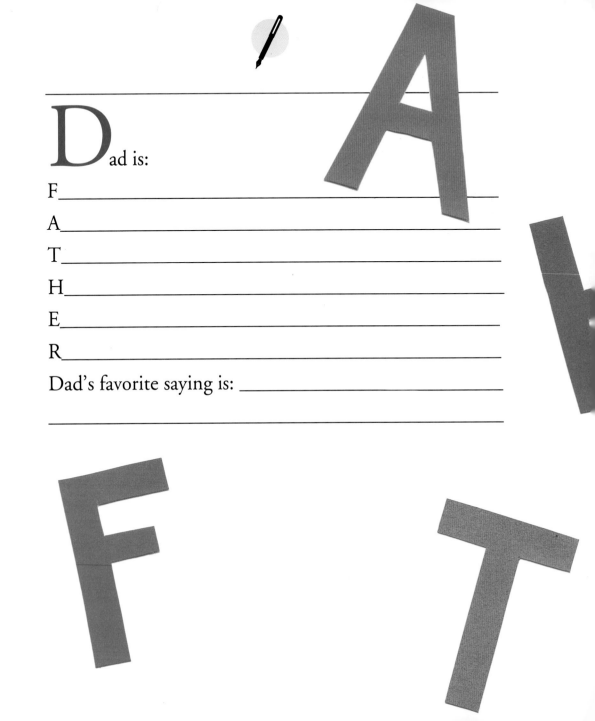

D~ad~ is:

F_____

A_____

T_____

H_____

E_____

R_____

Dad's favorite saying is: _____

_____

Design by Jenkins & Page, New York, NY.
Art Photography by Gamma One Conversions, New York, NY.
Composed in Adobe Garamond.
Type proofs by Graphic Arts Composition, Philadelphia, PA.
Printed and bound by Toppan Printing Company, Ltd., Singapore.